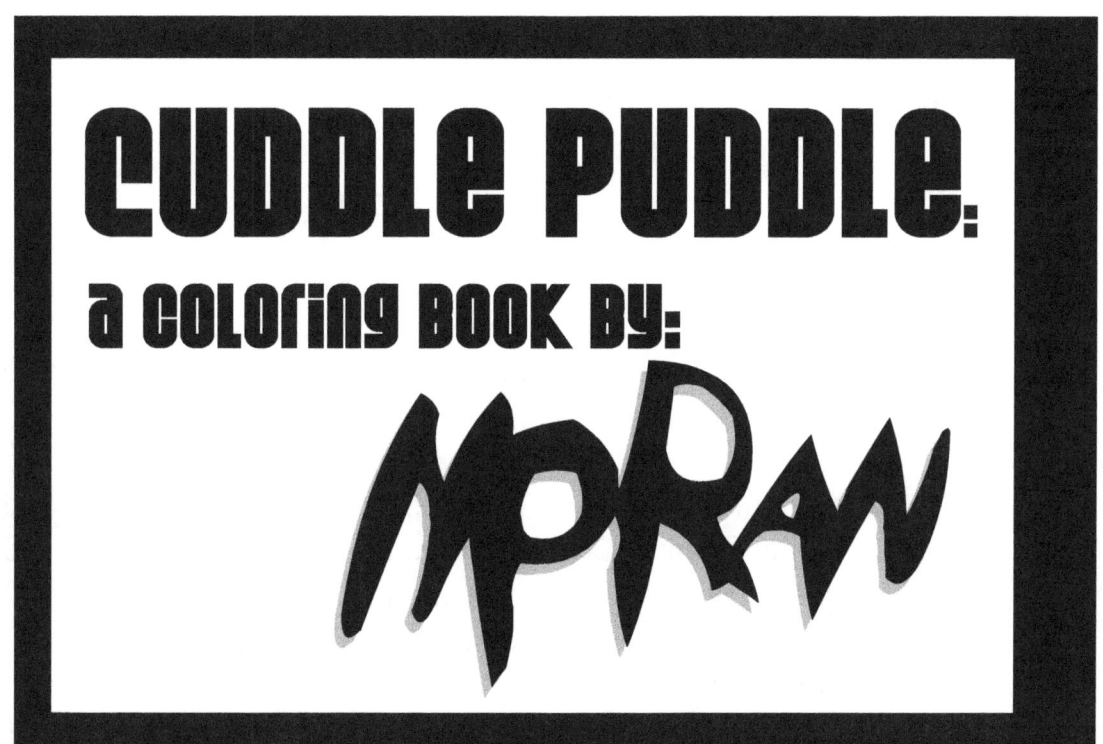

# CUDDLE PUDDLE:
## A COLORING BOOK BY: MORAN

# Table of Contents

**Drawings:**

Introduction:

    This book is a collection of drawings created over the past few years. The original art was created on location and often with the direct participation of the subjects featured. These drawings are a reflection of my life as an artist in the Western United States.

    With a blank sheet of paper, and using only pen and ink, I will sit for hours and render the world around me.

Ink blots and construction lines are the artifacts of this technique, I have chosen to preserve these imperfections where possible.

    This book would not be possible without the participation of the models and event producers that enrich my art life.

They deserve my special thanks and appreciation.

    I hope you enjoy this book and venture to color way outside of the lines.

    Thank you,

    Patrick J. Moran

Dedicated to my mother with thanks to:
Marcella

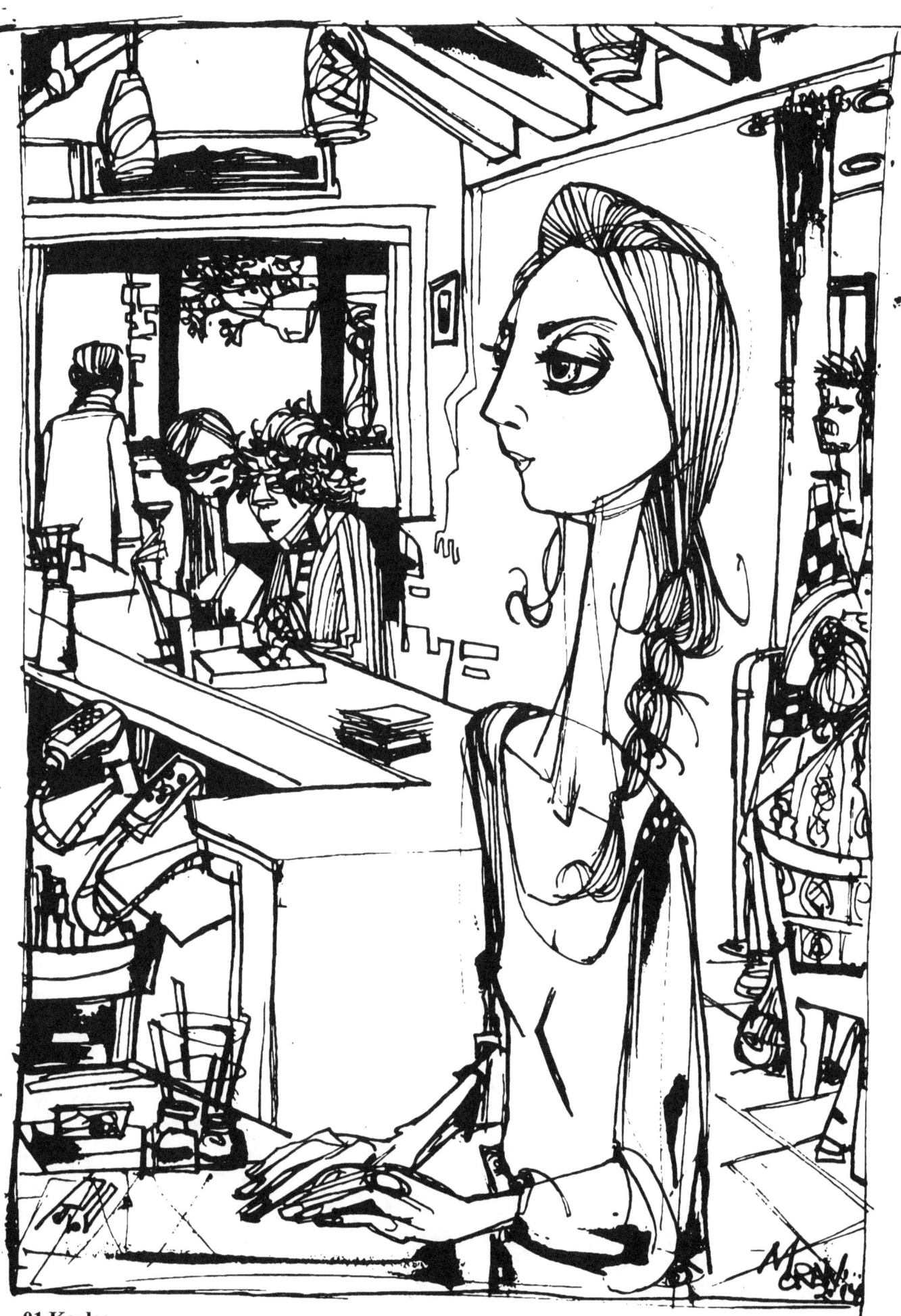

01 Kaylee

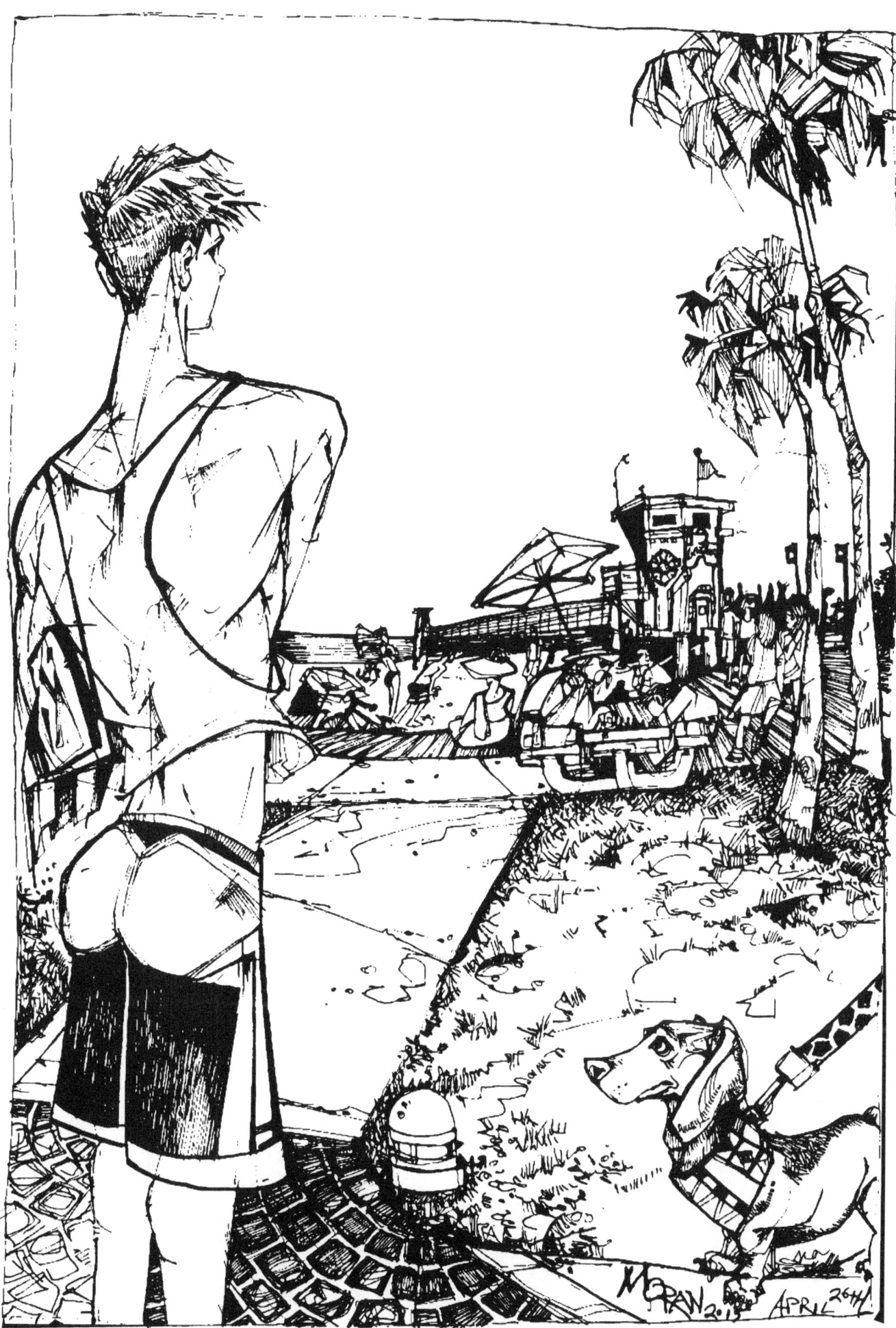

**02 Beach Bum**

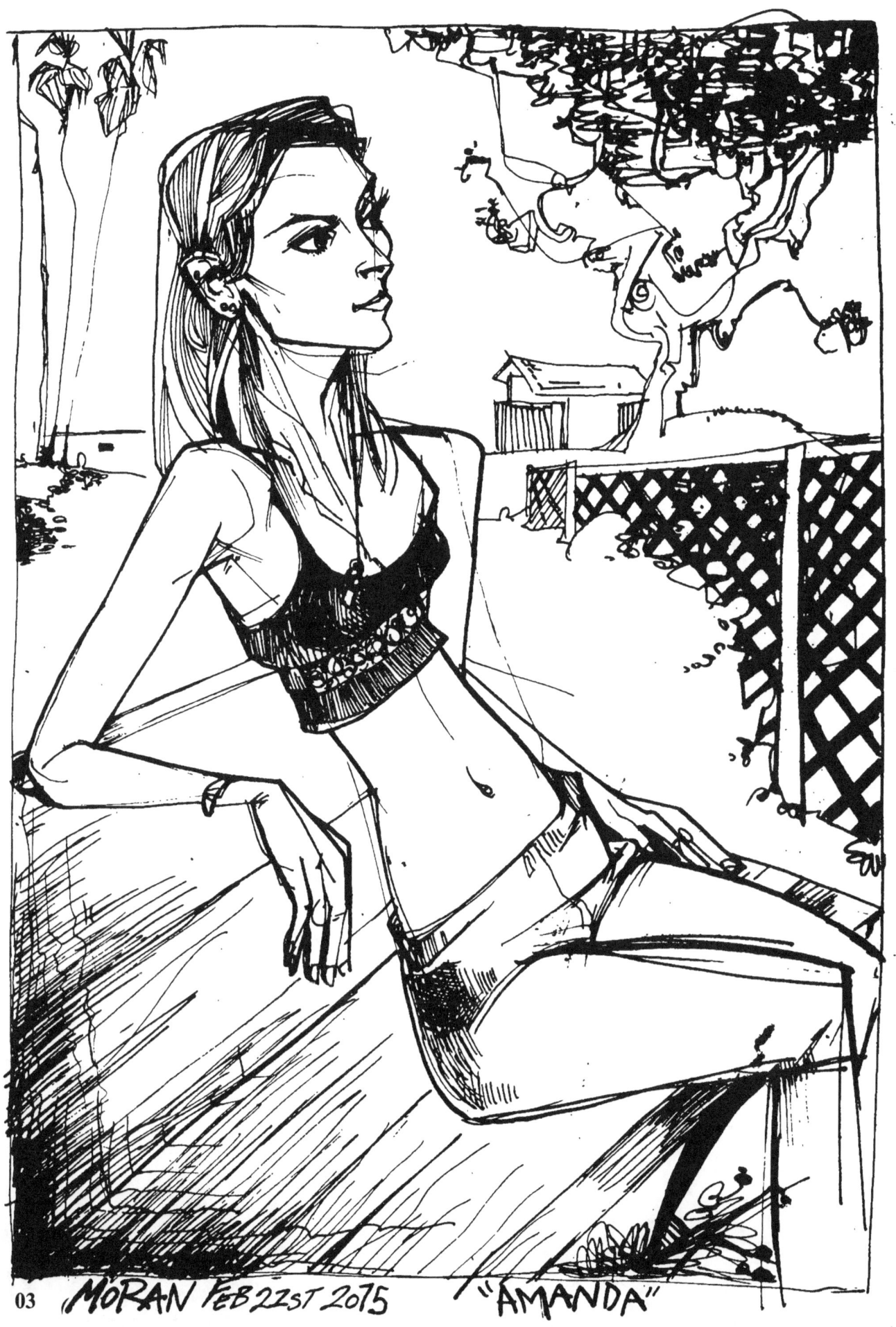

03 MORAN FEB 22st 2015 "AMANDA"

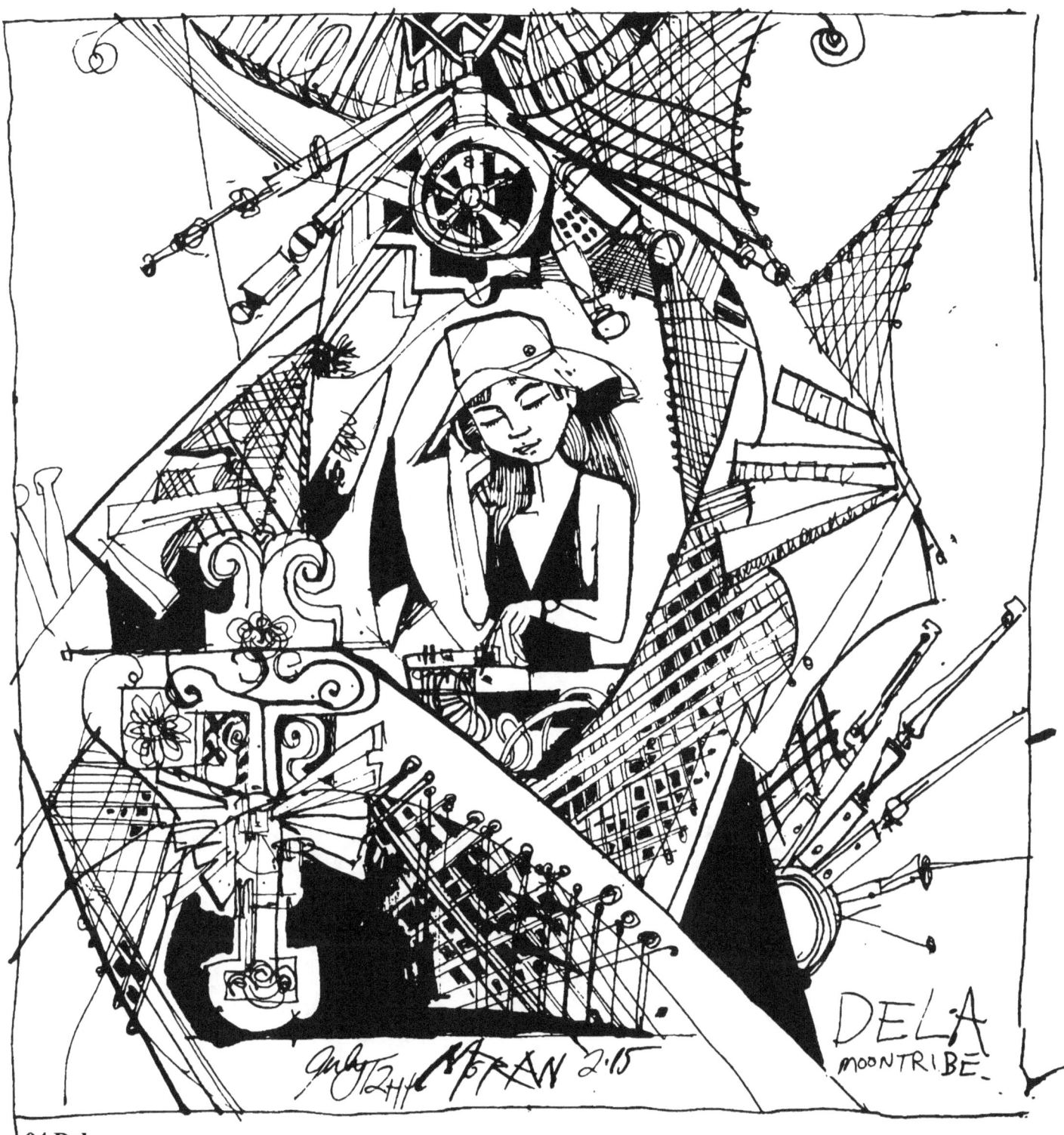

DELA
MOONTRIBE

04 Dela

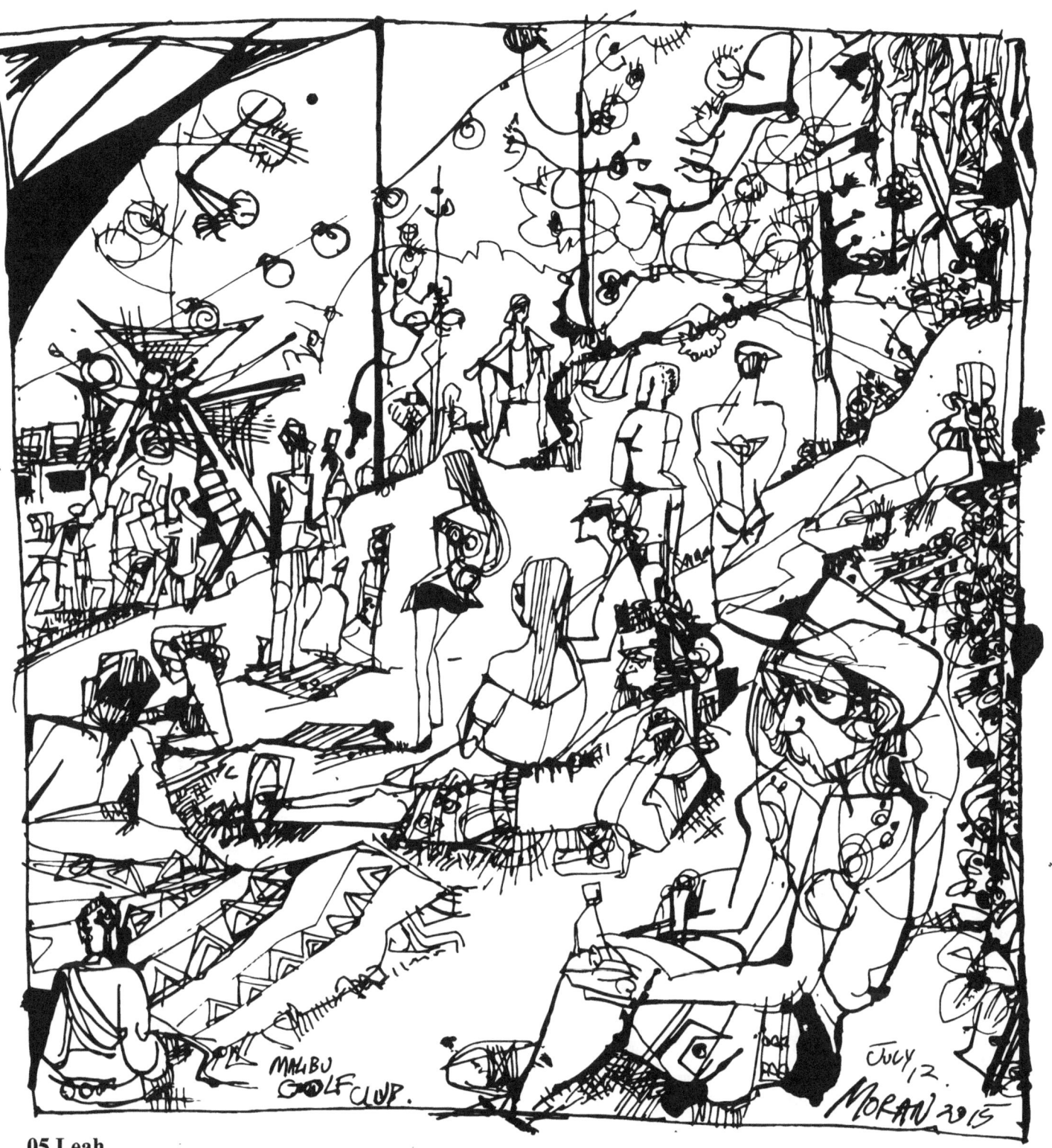

MALIBU
GOLF CLUB.

JULY, 12.

MORAN 2015

**05 Leah**

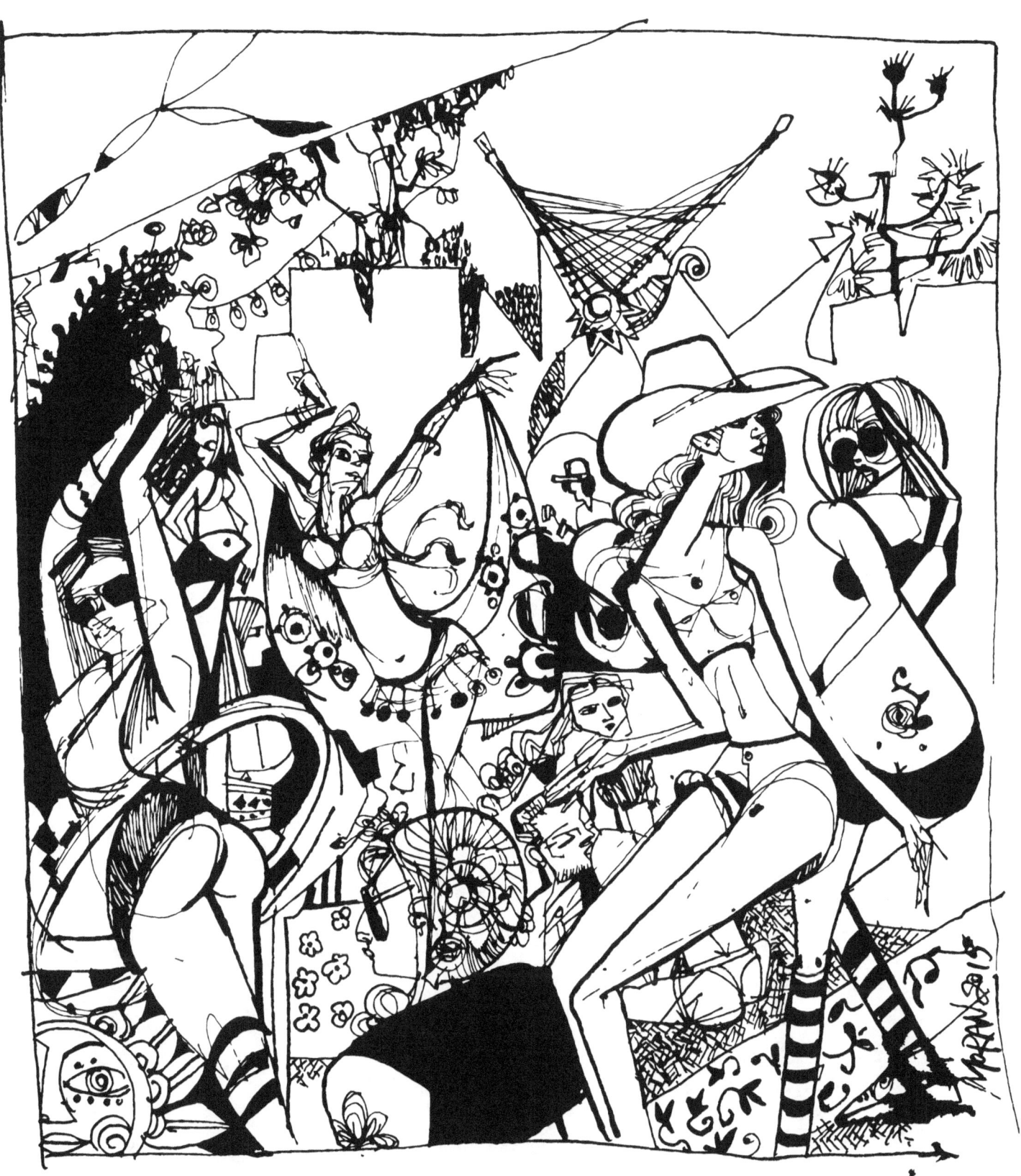

**06 Malibu Dance Party**

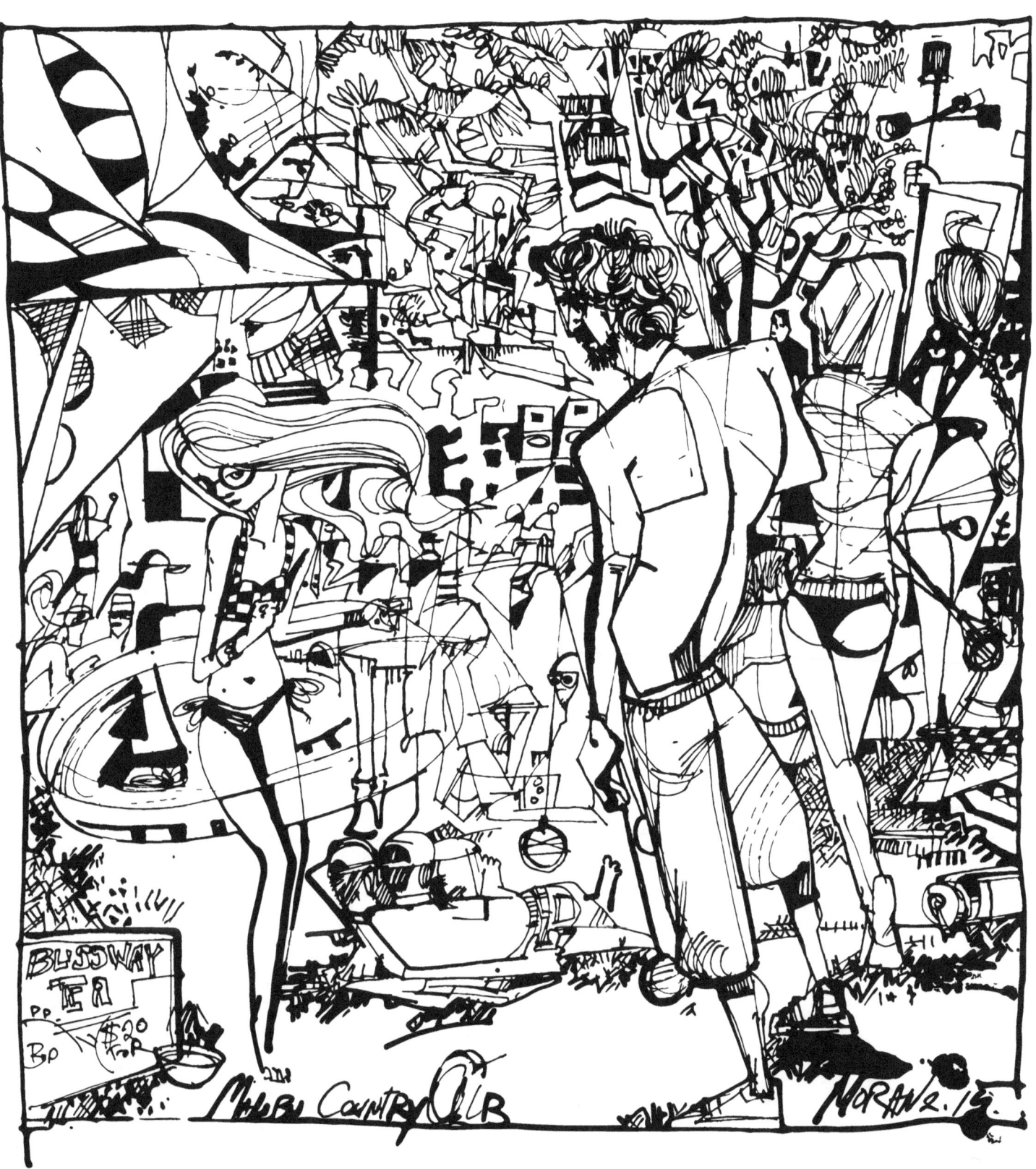

**07 Malibu Country Club**

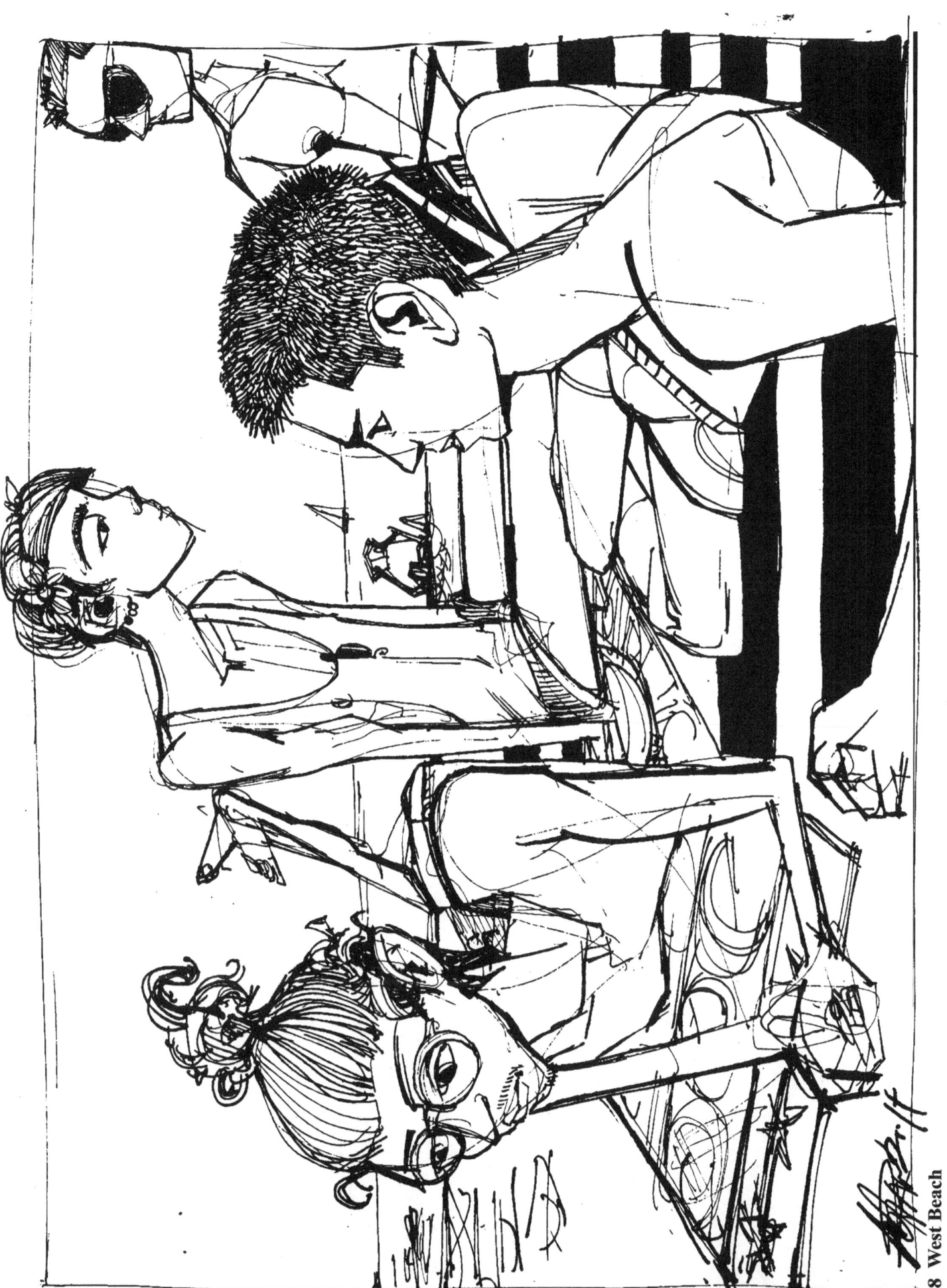

08 West Beach

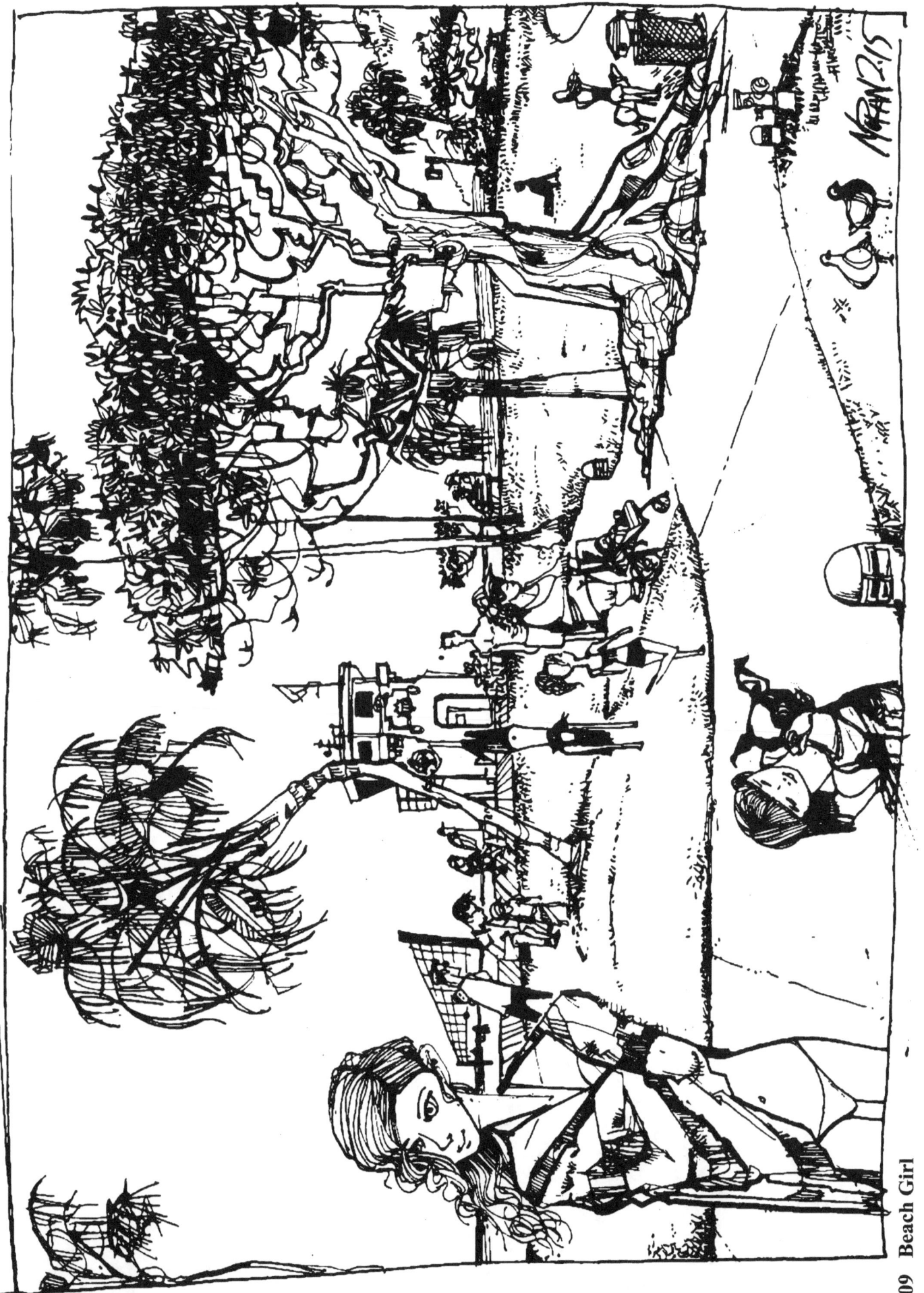

09  Beach Girl

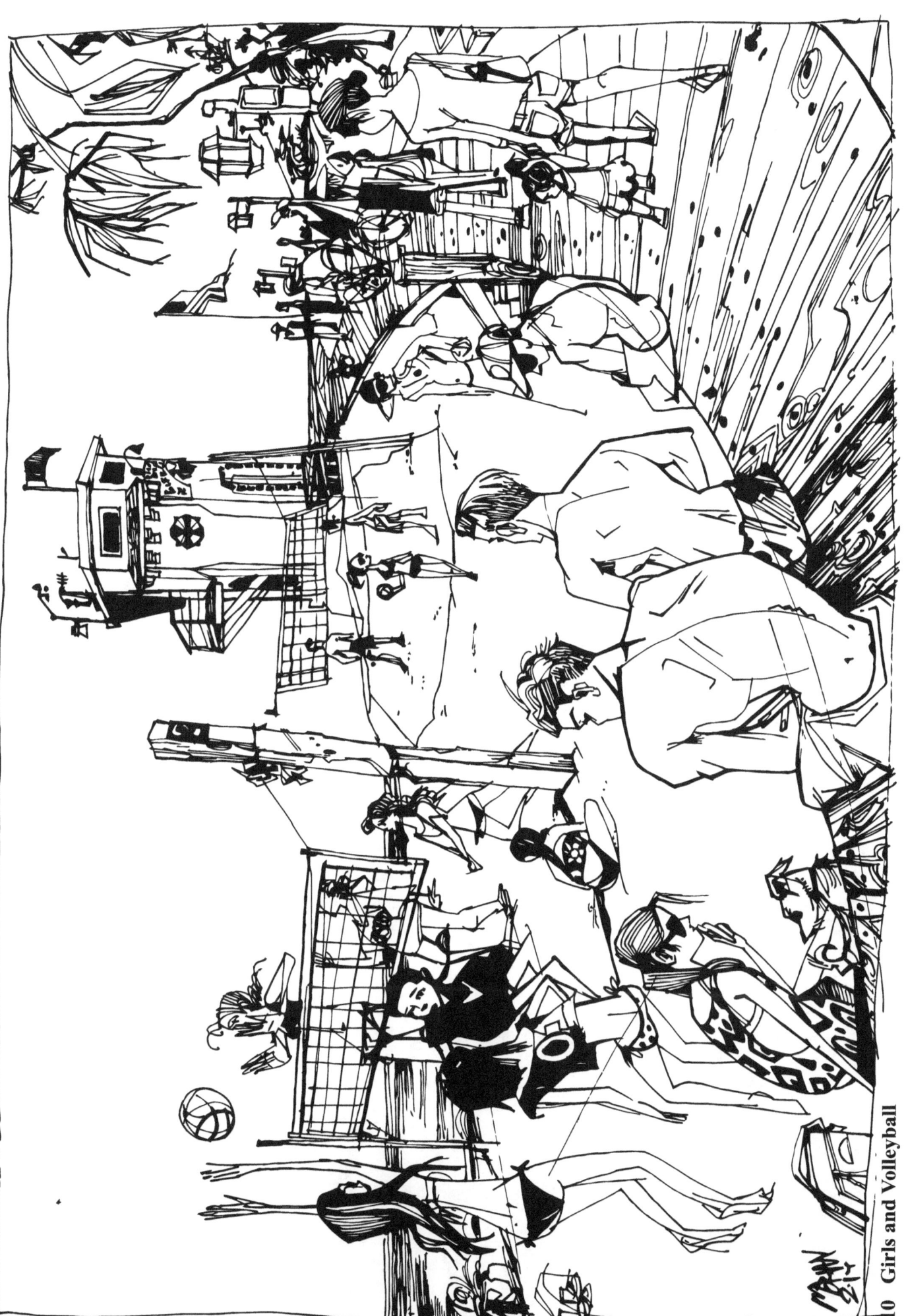

10  Girls and Volleyball

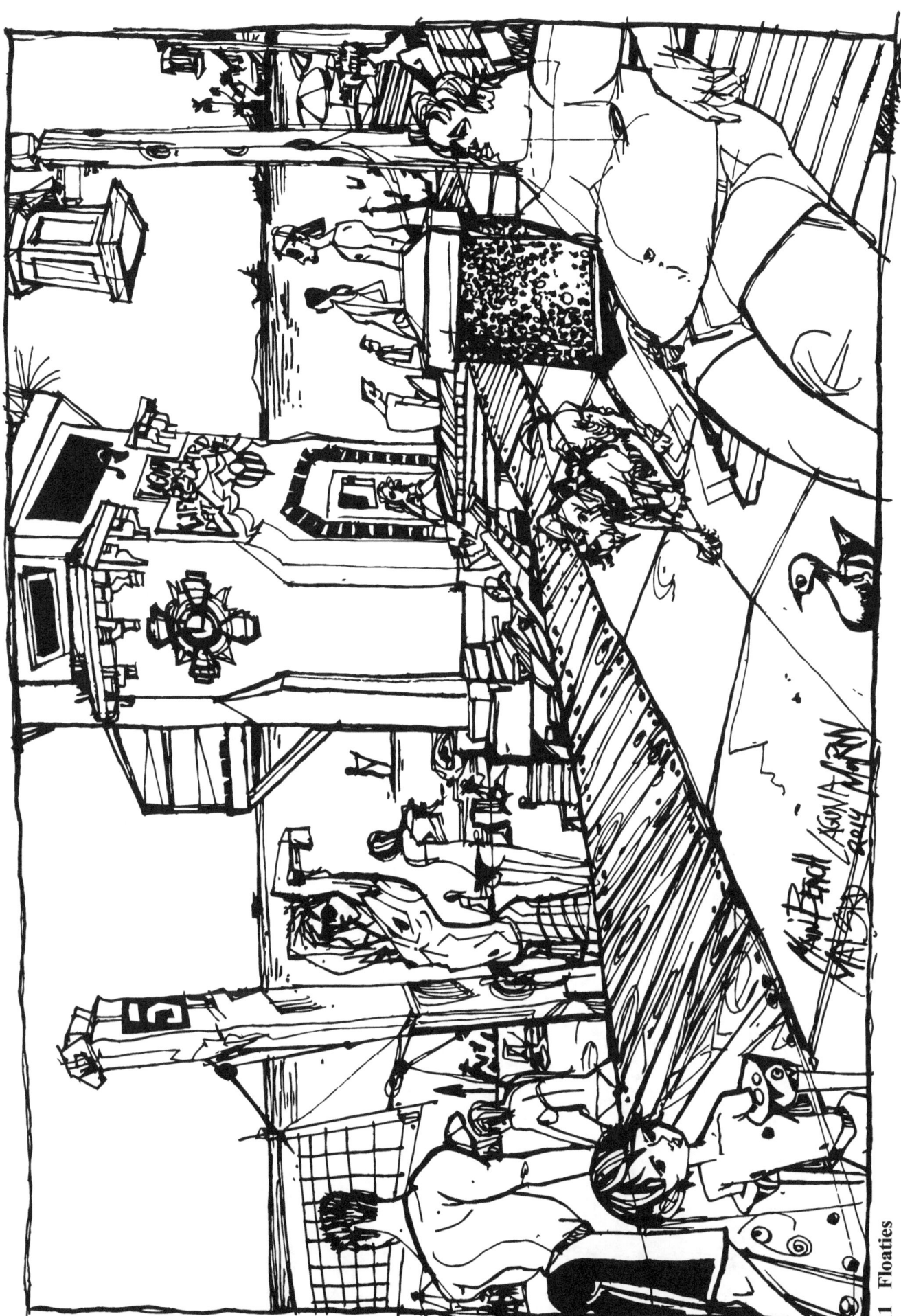

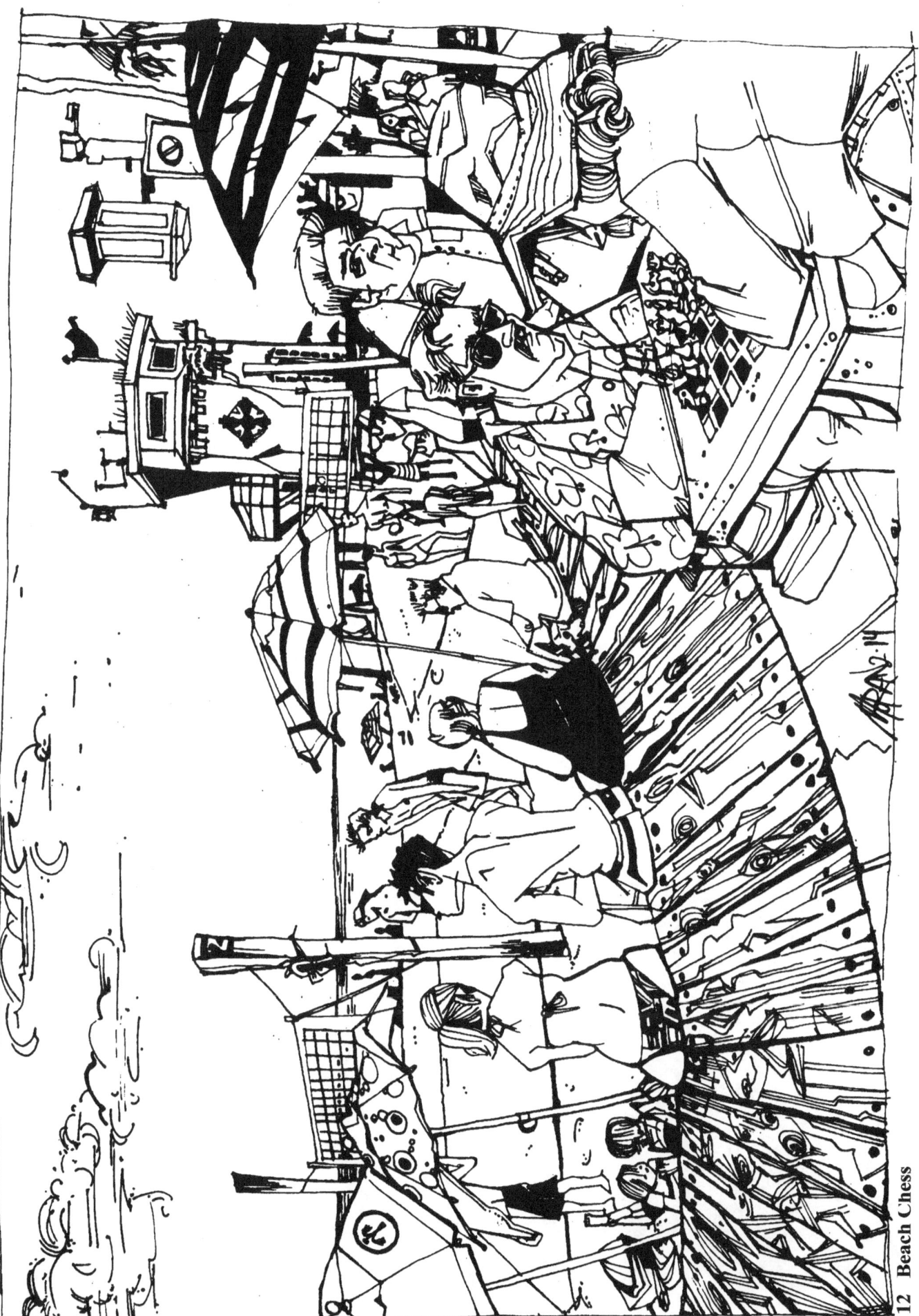

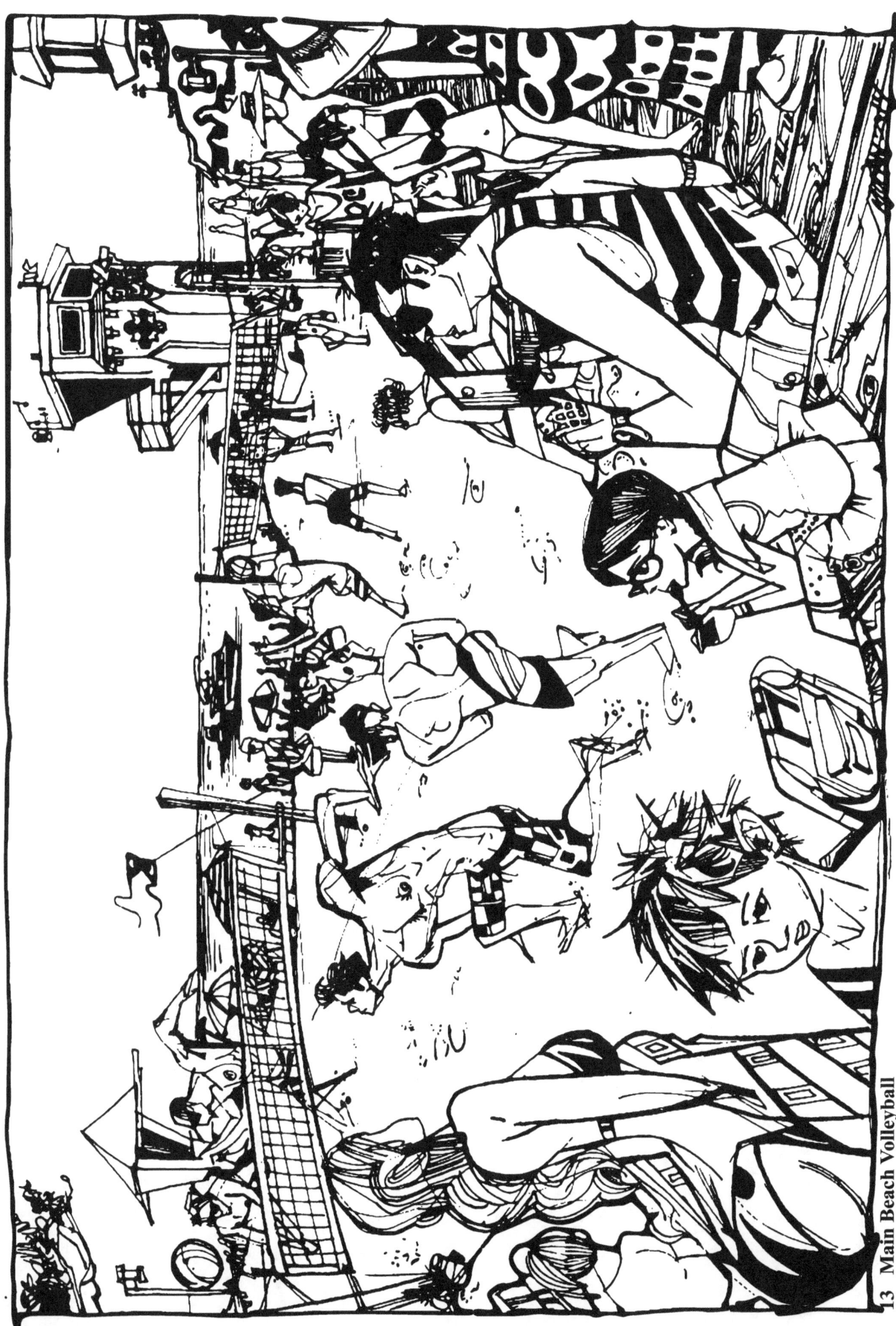

13  Main Beach Volleyball

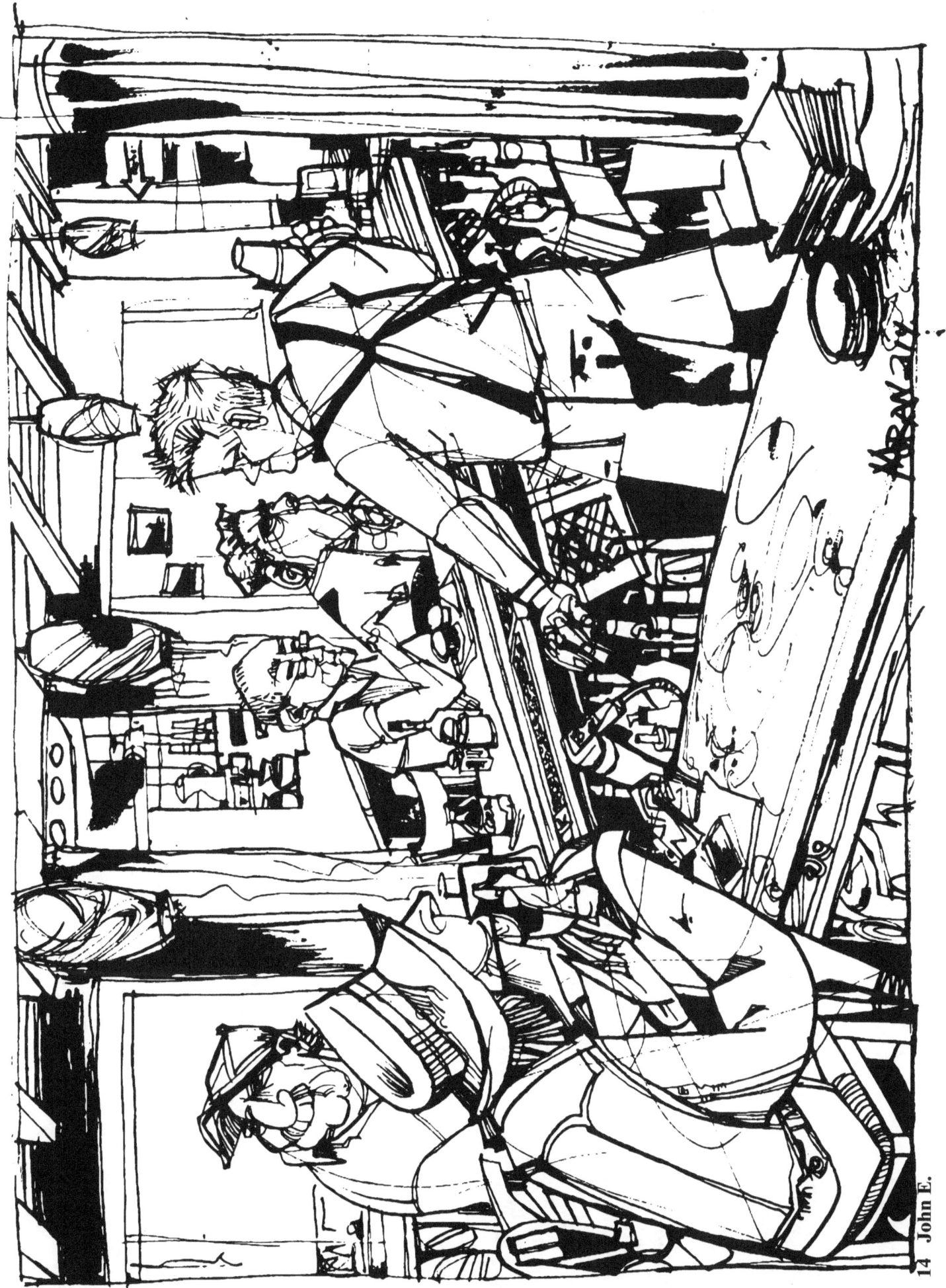

14  John E.

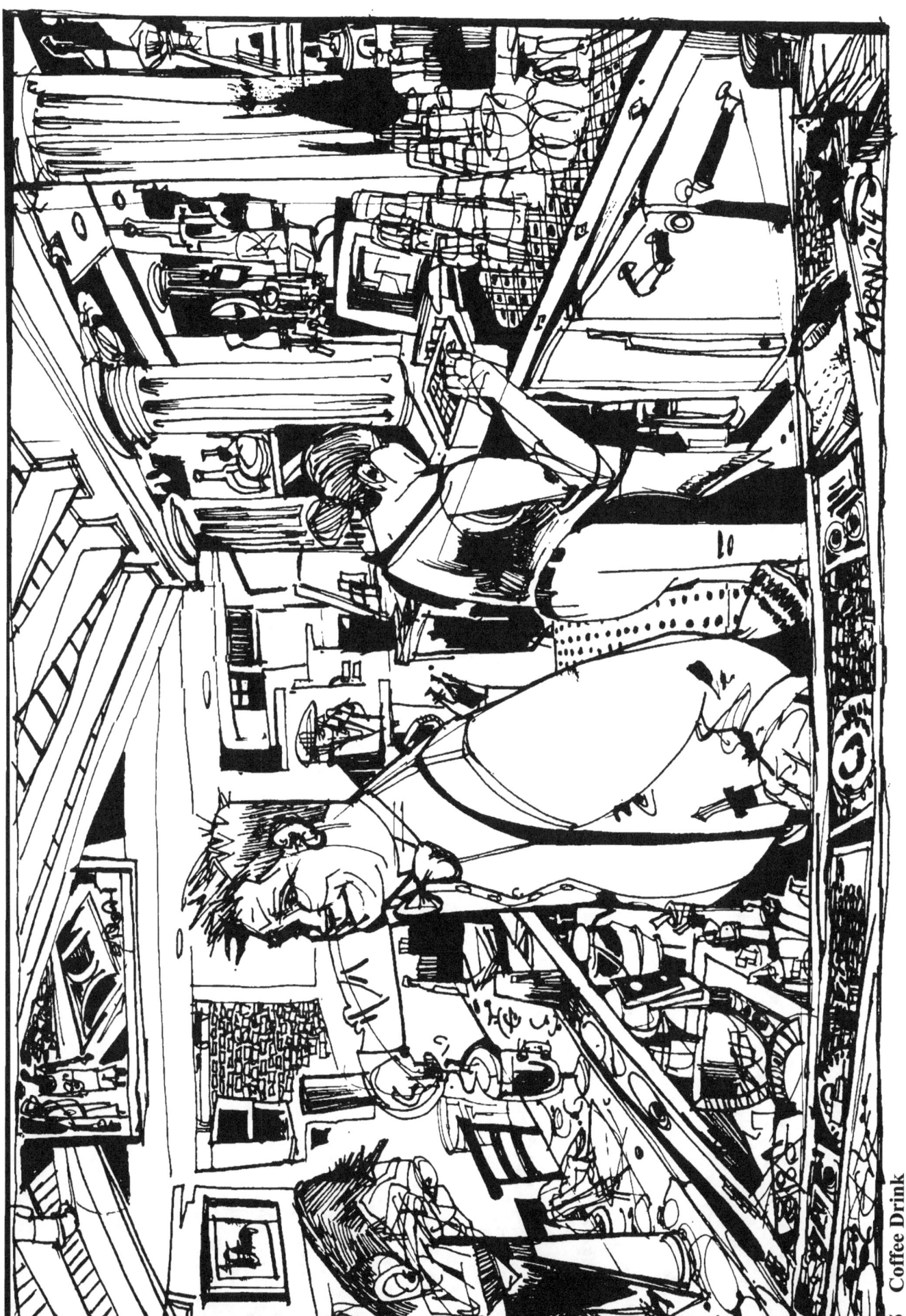

15  Coffee Drink

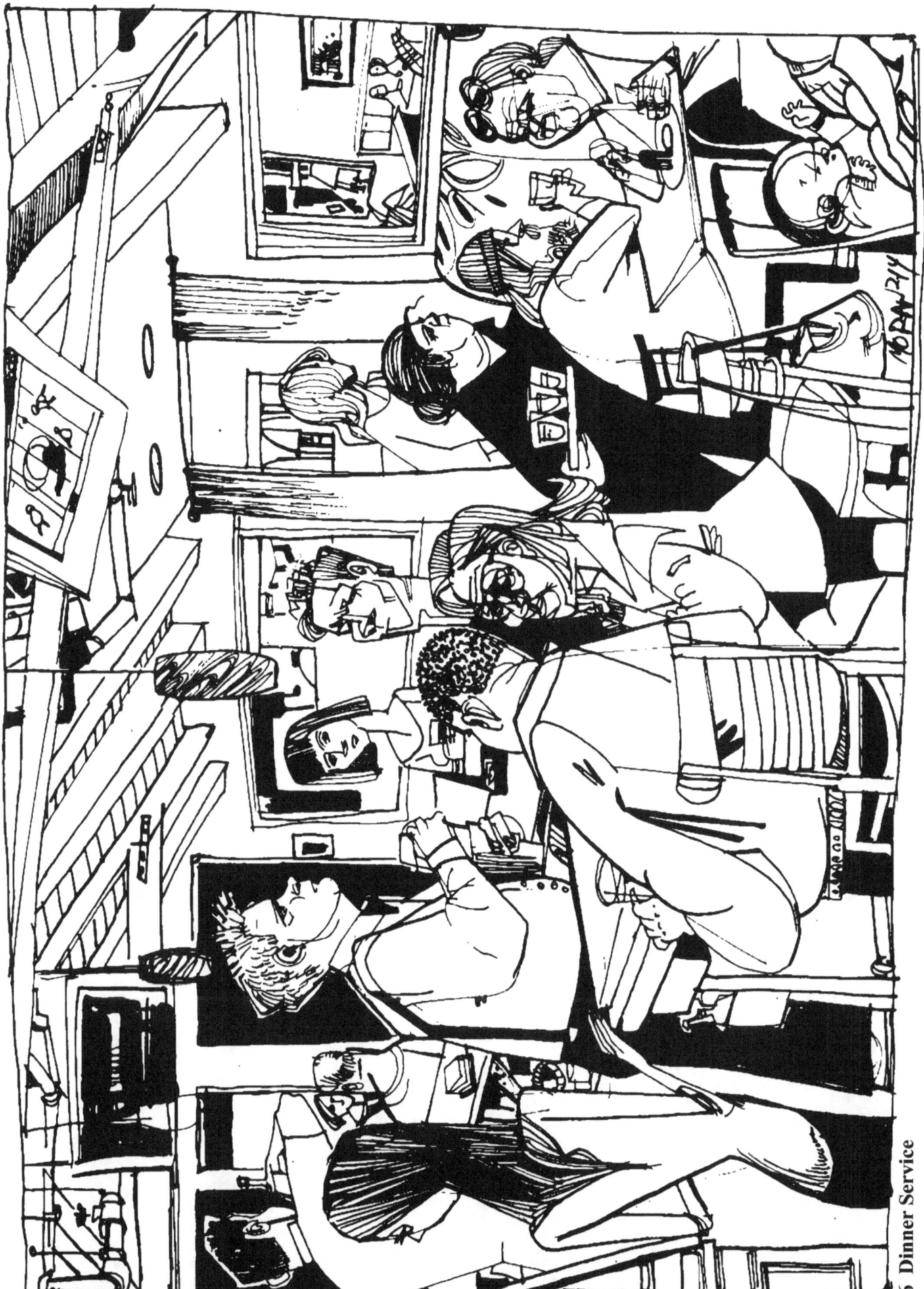

16 Dinner Service

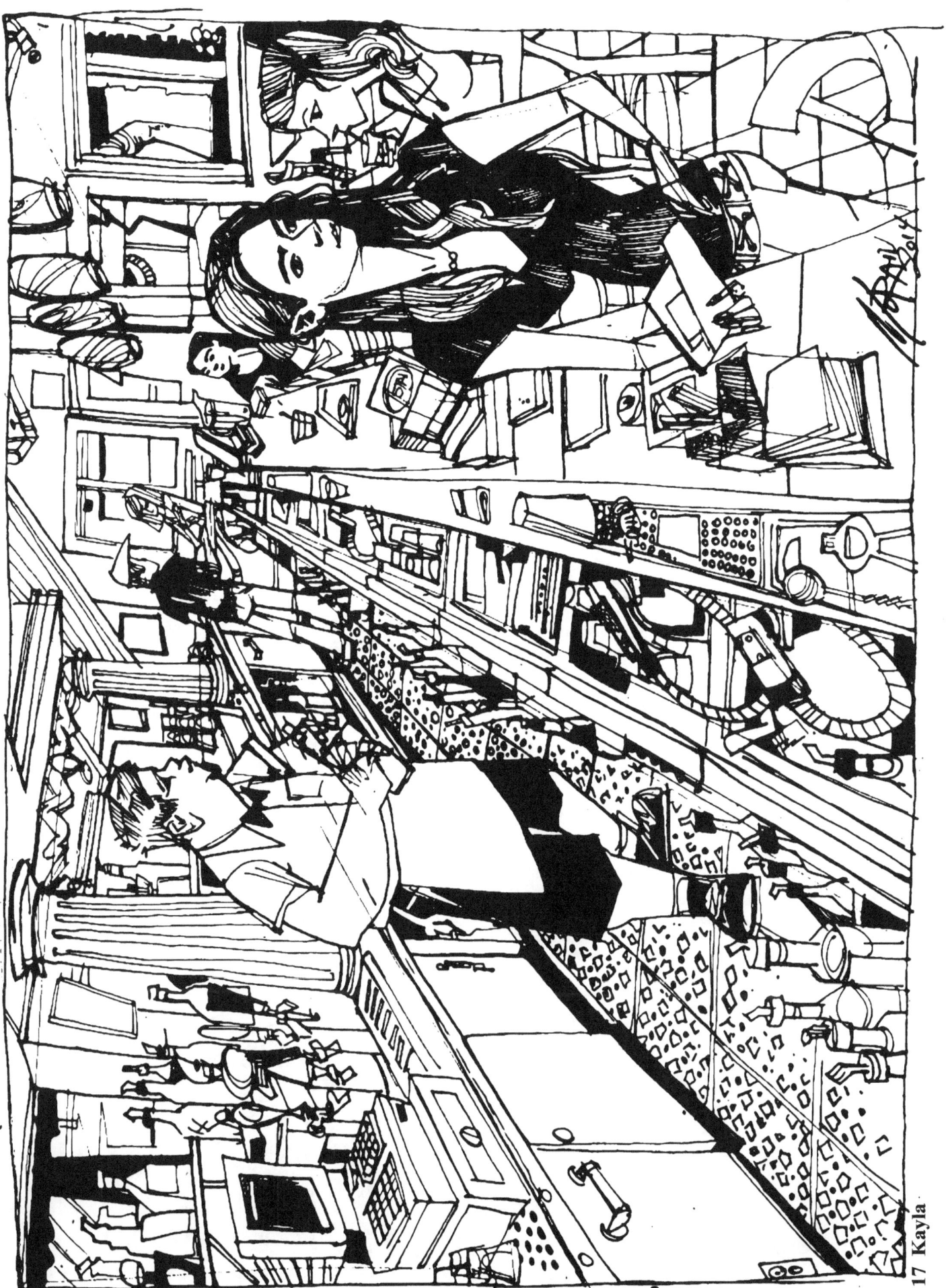

17 Kayla

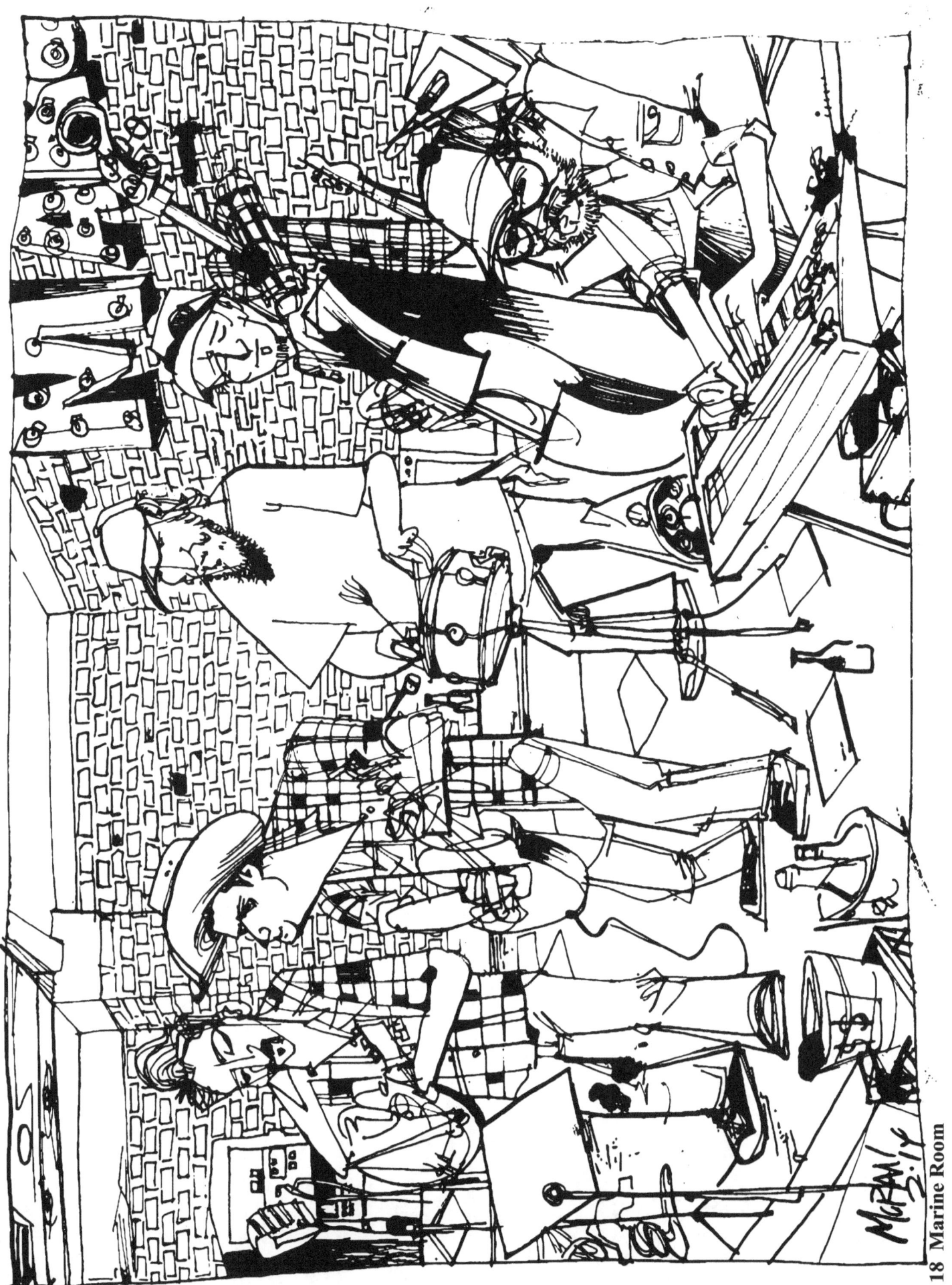

18  Marine Room

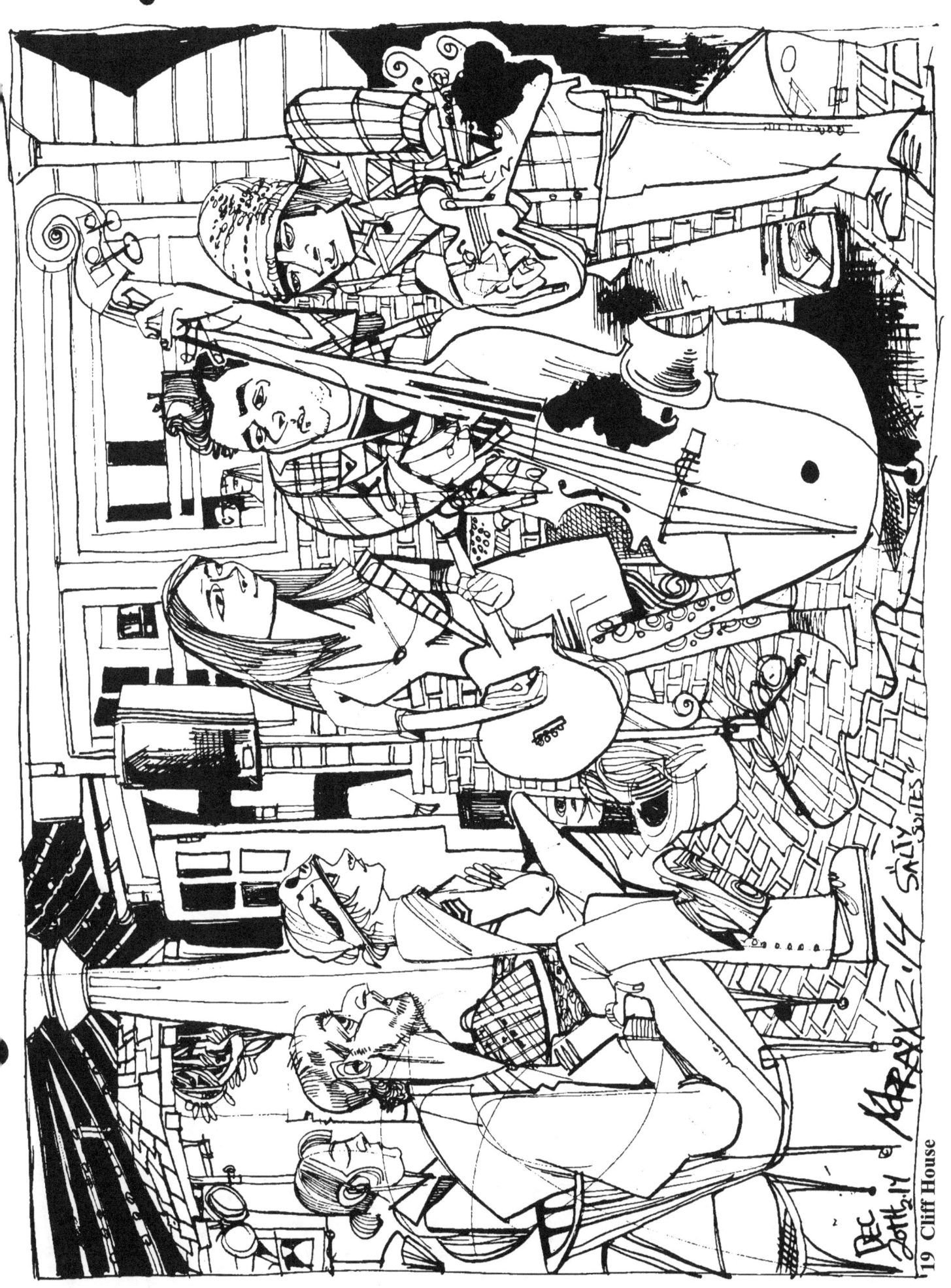

19 Cliff House

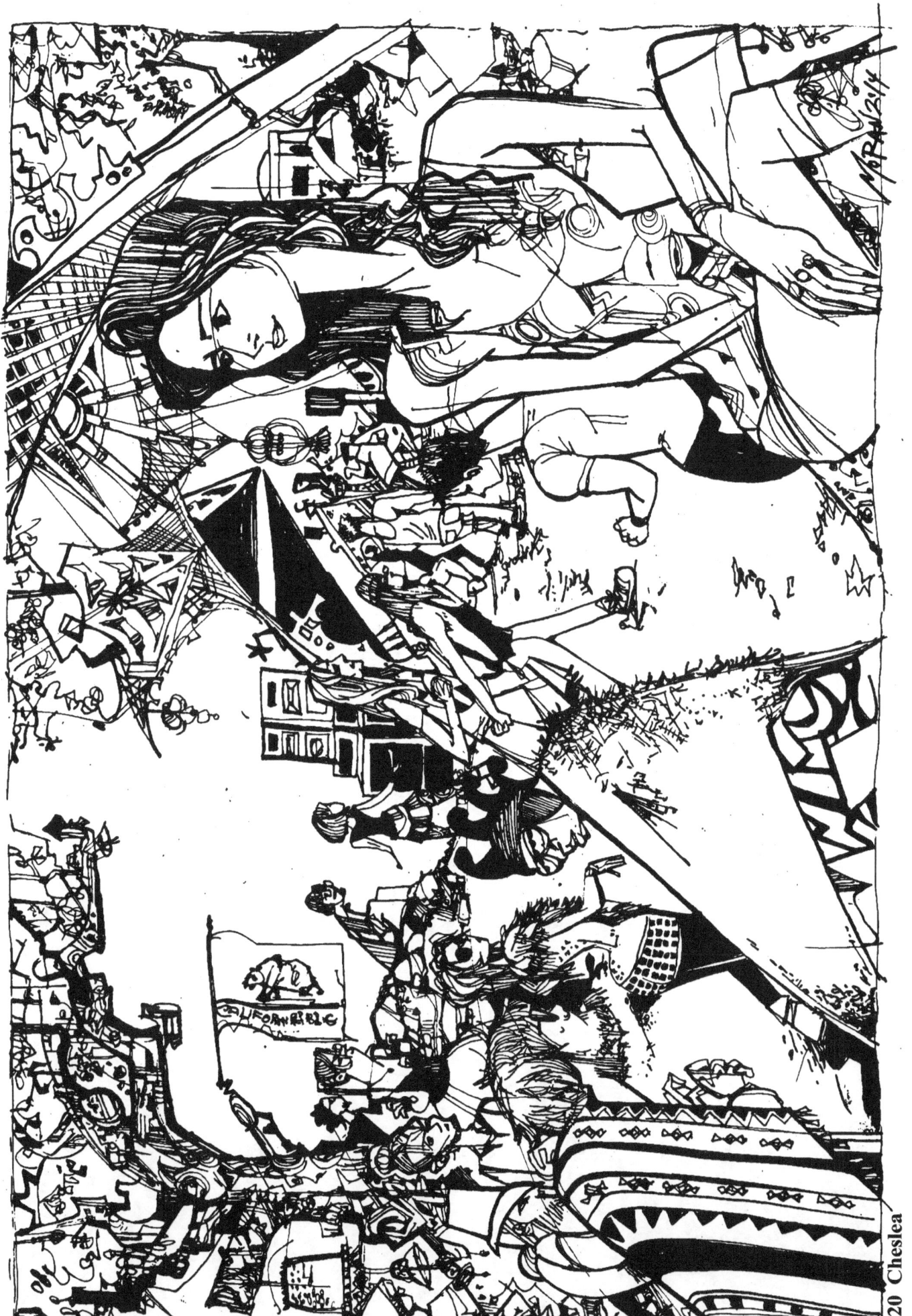

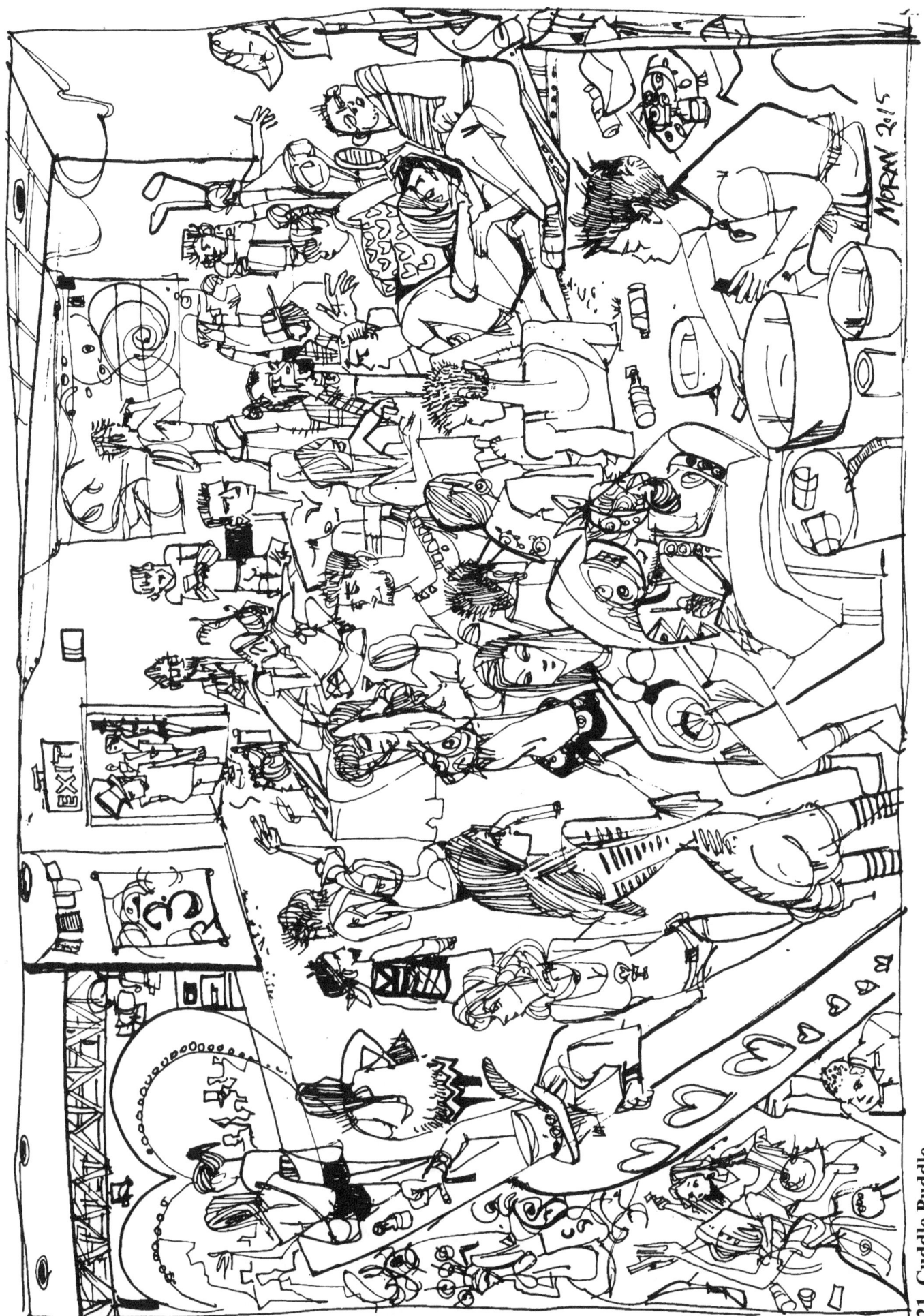

21 Cuddle Puddle

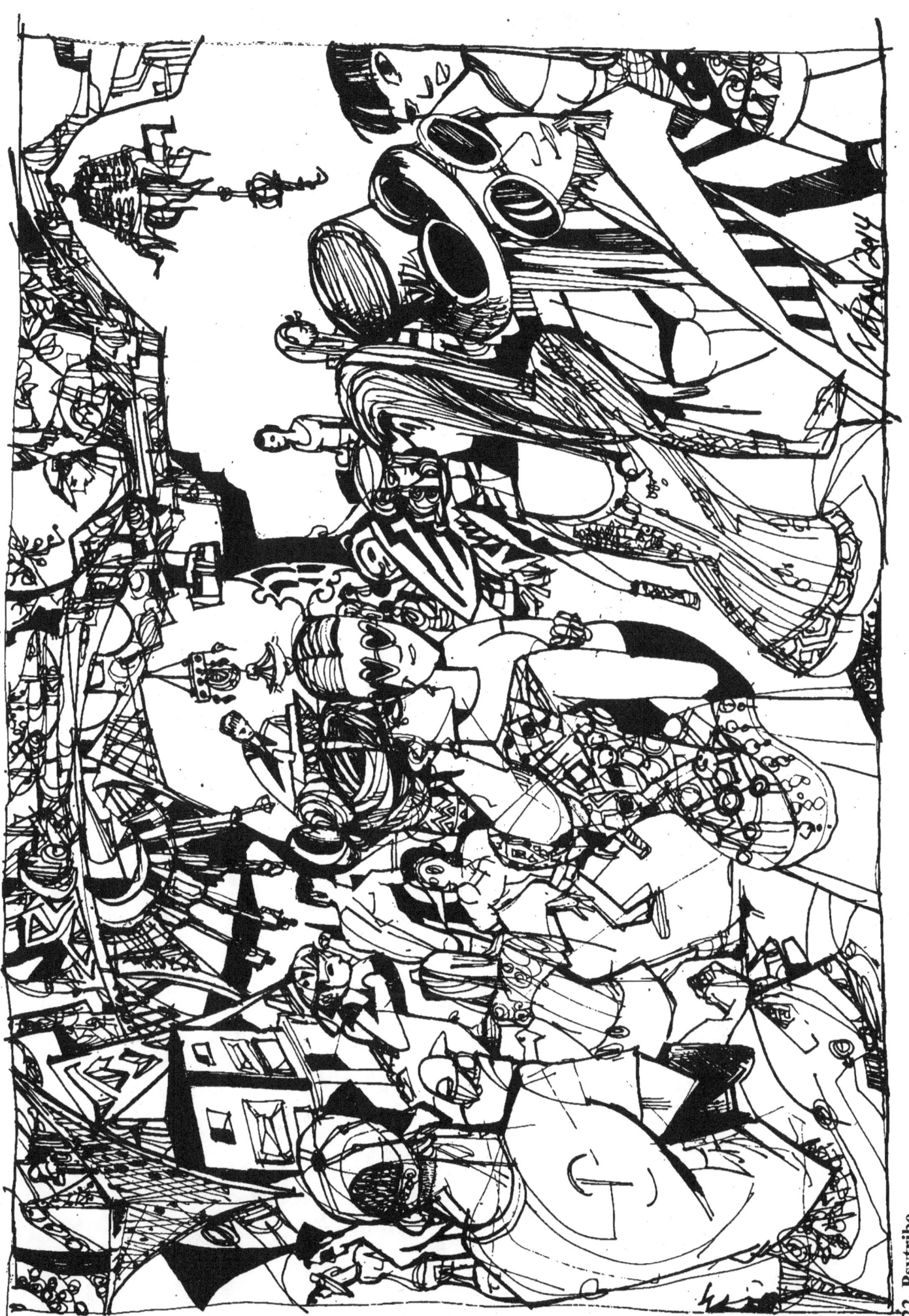

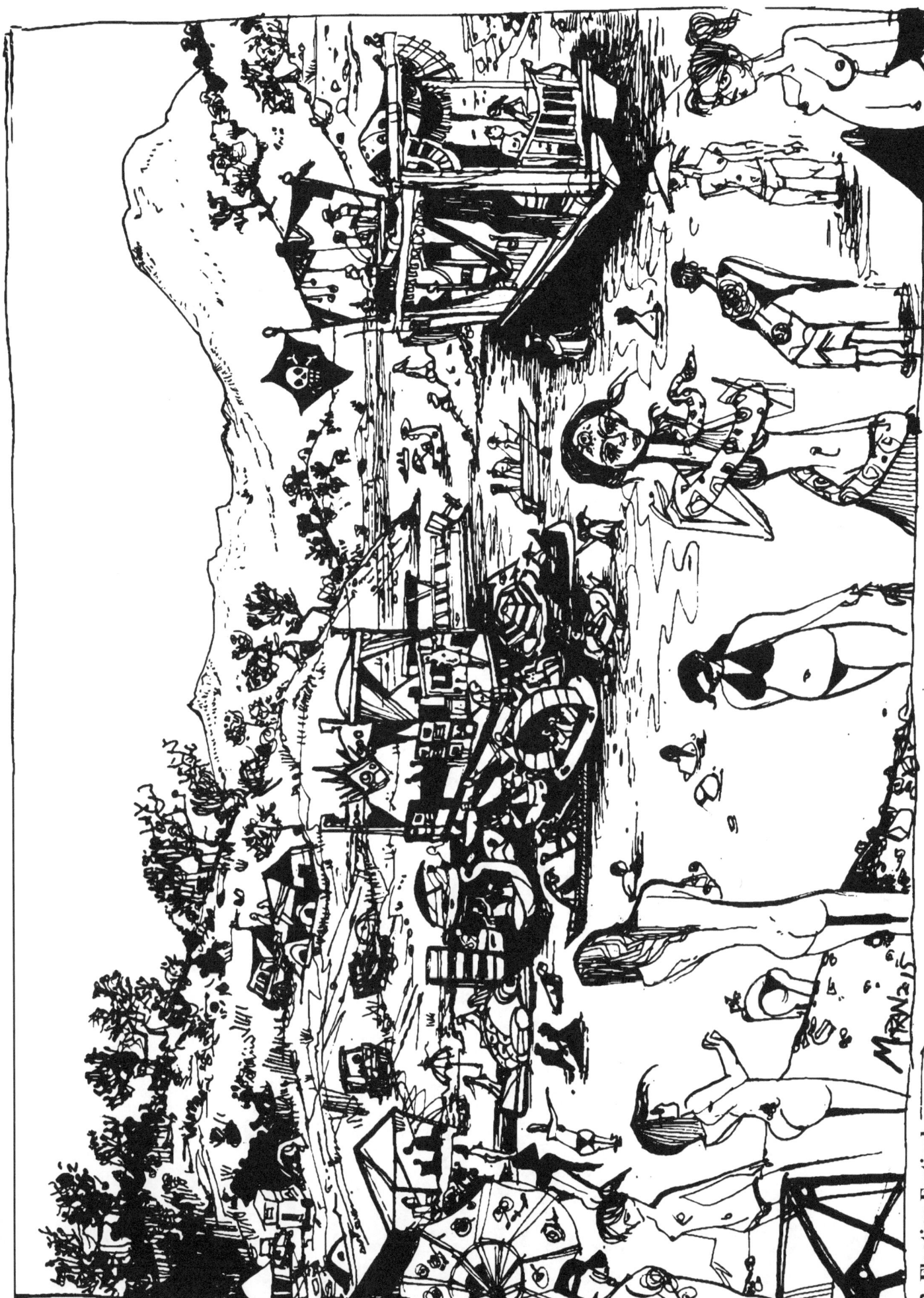

23 Floating Festival

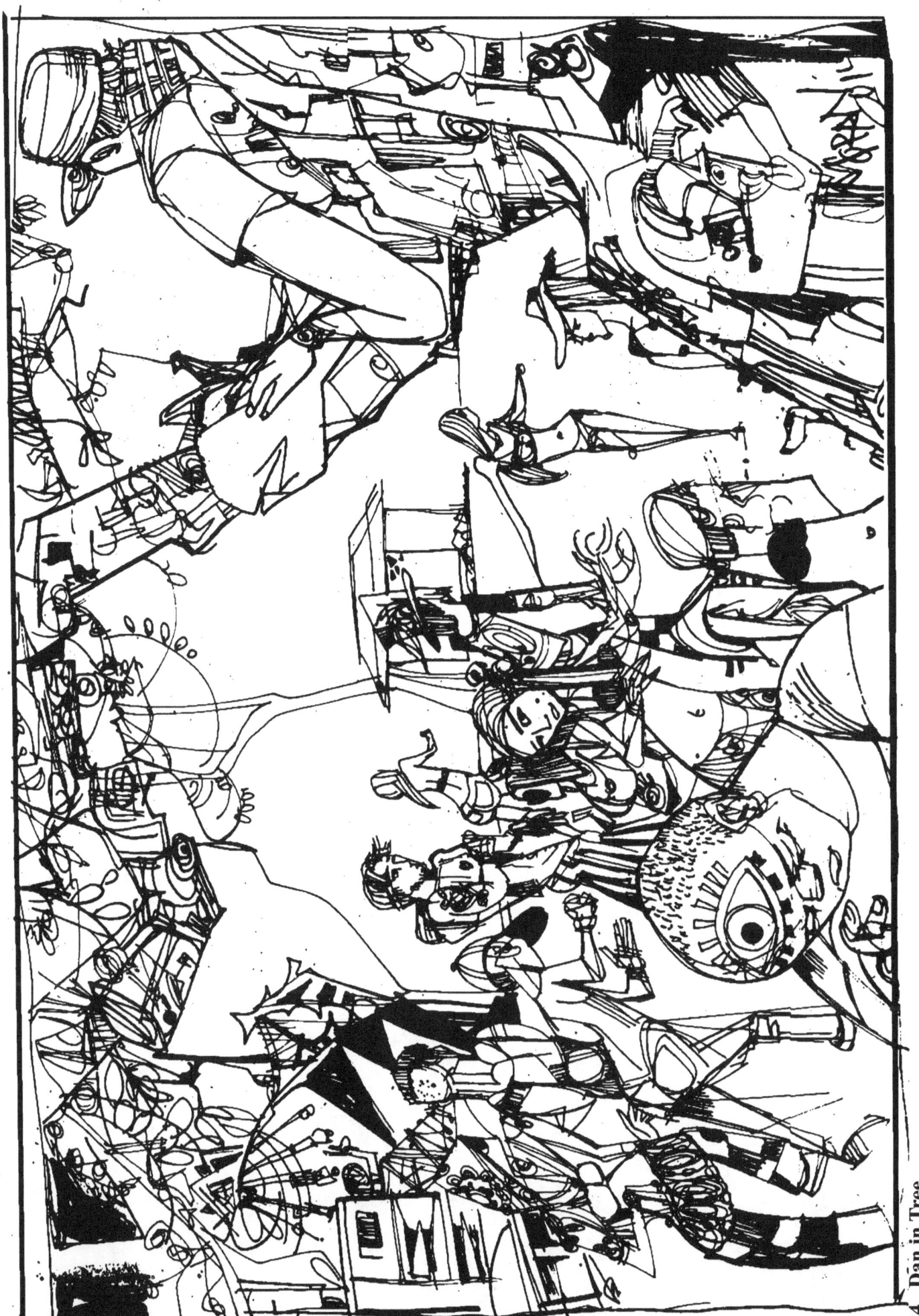

24 Dan in Tree

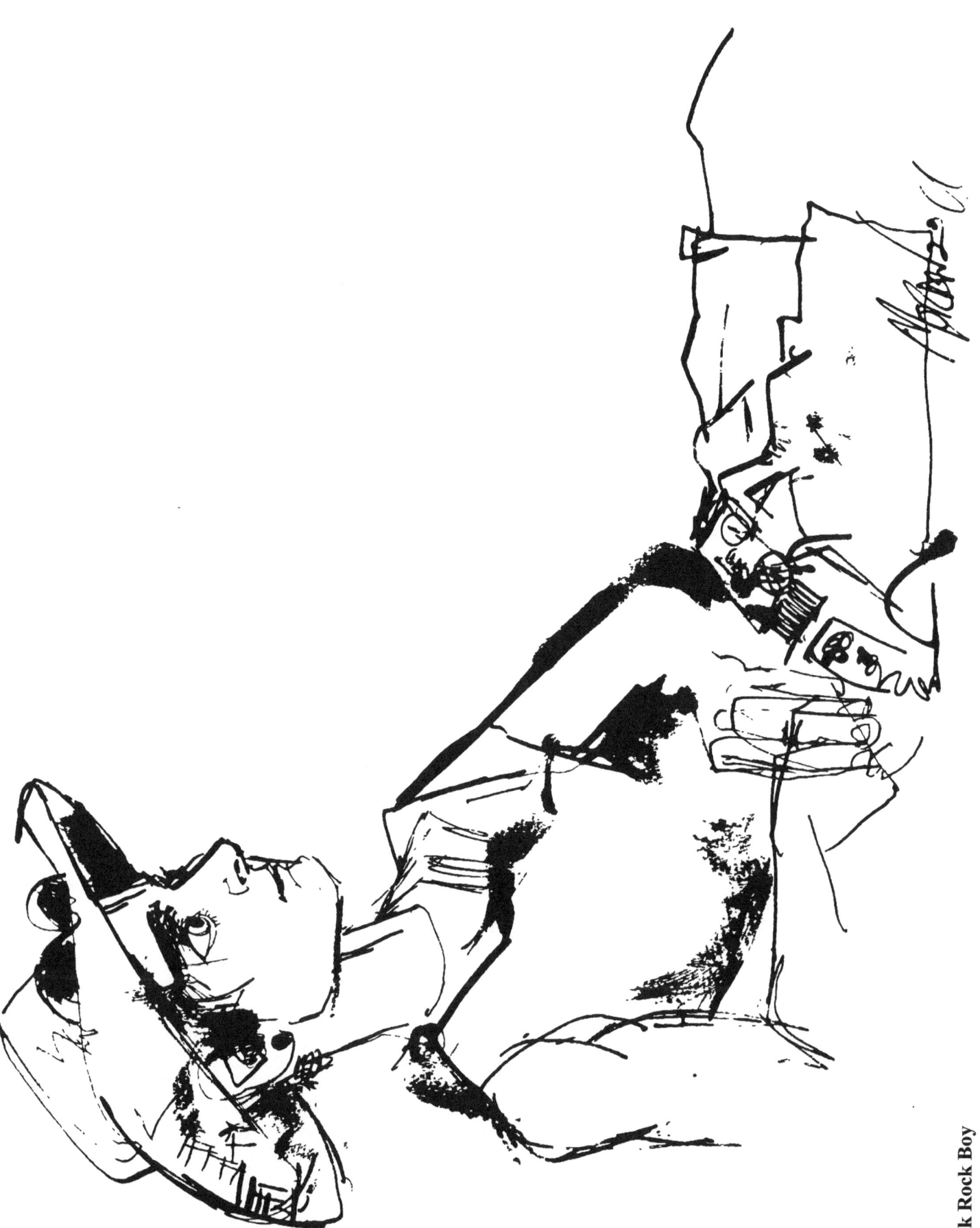

25 Black Rock Boy

www.ingramcontent.com/pod-product-compliance
Lightning Source LLC
Chambersburg PA
CBHW080611180526
45168CB00007B/2872